A TRIBUTE TO THE ADVERTISING AGENCY THE

LONDON PRESS EXCHANGE

THE UNSUNG LEADER OF THE FIELD

RUTH ARTMONSKY

A TRIBUTE TO THE ADVERTISING AGENCY THE

LONDON PRESS EXCHANGE
THE UNSUNG LEADER OF THE FIELD

RUTH ARTMONSKY

Published by:
Artmonsky Arts
Flat 1, 27 Henrietta Street
London WC2E 8NA
artmonskyruth@gmail.com
Tel. 07767 820 406

Text © Ruth Artmonsky 2024

ISBN 978-1-7385016-0-1

Designed by:
David Preston Studio
www.davidprestonstudio.com

Printed in Wales by:
Gomer Press
https://gomerprinting.co.uk

My thanks to my exceptional researcher Stella Harpley, to Eduardo Sant'Anna for his help with the illustrations, and to my loyal forbearing designer David Preston for parcelling my text and illustrations into an attractive bundle. The cover is in homage to David's mentor Phil Baines whose untimely death occurred early this year.

Contents

Introduction	06
The London Press Exchange	08
Artists & Designers	16
Sample Adverts	26
Consumer Research	40
Sample Campaigns	47
Mr Mercury	48
Mr Therm	54
The Squander Bug	60
The Little Man	66
'Top People'	72
Epilogue	76

INTRODUCTION

St. Martin's Lane, in Westminster, had originally been a mere country byway linking the church of St. Martin's-in-the-Fields with that of St. Giles-in-the-Fields. By the twentieth century a company's publicity brochure described it as, 'a queer colour place, this St. Martin's Lane. Courts and alleys traverse it. In these you find bookshops and curios'.

But contemporary Londoners, nowadays, might see it more as the eastern border of theatre land, with the Noel Coward and Duke of York on one side, and the Coliseum lower down on the opposite side. A select small band of connoiseurs of furniture history might remark that the road had once been where the Chippendales, father and son, had lived and had their workshop. But it would be a mere handful of people, enthusiasts of advertising history, who would be able to record that it was in St. Martin's Lane, at NOS. 108–112, that there was once the largest advertising agency in Britain; and of that handful hardly one would be likely to be able to name its founder, one Reginald James Sykes.

Why, in the history of British advertising in its formative years, has the London Press Exchange and its entrepreneurial founder Sykes, been so unwarrantedly neglected, when the likes of William Crawford and Charles Higham, with their sizeable egos, but less sizable operations, have tended to dominate the scene. A superficial argument, might be that its title, the London Press Exchange, is not immediately recognisable as an advertising

Reginald James Sykes, Founder and Chairman of the London Press Exchange, c. 1936.

agency, when its contemporary agencies would, like firms of lawyers, be known by the names of their proprietors – as F.C. Pritchard Wood and Partners Ltd or Colman, Prentis and Varley. But a more substantial reason could well be that it had a clear policy not to advertise itself.

An unidentified director of the agency, in *Art & Industry* in September 1950, spelt it out:

> Our policy has always been one of considerable reticence, in that we do not utilize either the general or trade press to advertise ourselves, though special advertisements may occasionally appear in some trade papers, issued by one or other of the subsidiary companies.

Here we set out to redress the situation, to belatedly, in hindsight, parade, on behalf of the London Press Exchange, its exploits that led it to dominate the British advertising world (both by its size and in its profitability) in the first half of the twentieth century.

THE LONDON PRESS EXCHANGE

Major George Harrison, Managing Director of the London Press Exchange, c. 1961.

It was in 1892 that two young reporters, Reginald James Sykes and Frederick Higginbottom, decided to set up a business to supply news items, particularly on sport, to provincial newspapers. They established themselves first in a room in Fleet Street, then moving to Charing Cross, and finally settling in St. Martin's Lane – the moves perhaps symbolizing the change of focus of the company.

As Sykes began to transform himself from reporter to advertising man, Higginbottom seems to have decided to remain in journalism, having a spell with the *Pall Mall Gazette* (for a short time as its editor), before joining the *Daily Chronicle* where he remained until his retirement in 1930. LPE was left in the hands of Sykes alone; and it was Sykes and his three sons – Reginald Charles, Richard Lawrence and Anthony – who were to hold the reins, at one level or another, for much of LPE's existence.

Reginald James remained the agency's Chairman until he died in 1940; Reginald Charles, the oldest son, who had joined the agency in 1922, became its Chairman and Managing Director in 1961; Richard Lawrence became his Vice-Chairman. It is intriguing that none of the sons were considered ready, immediately, to succeed their father, a position taken up by one, George Harrison.

Reginald James was, indeed, a hard act to follow, for not only had he founded the agency and was the controlling hand, but became for two periods (1929-31 and 1934-7) the President of the Institute of Practitioners in Advertising, a Council member and later Treasurer of the Advertising Association, and Vice-President of the

National Advertising Benevolent Association. He had made himself into an advertising man through and through .The 'reticence' that has been ascribed to LPE policy, certainly did not imply any social distancing from its founder, for not only was Sykes active in his various professional bodies, but is recorded as something of a club man, with riding and golf said to be his main means of relaxation.

In 1936 *Commercial Art* chose Sykes to be first in its series 'key men in advertising':

> To hear him talk about advertising is to see his enthusiasm for his subject; and to ask him only a few questions about it is to realize how thoroughly he knows his ground.

In the same article Sykes' valuation of his industry's contribution to society was astounding:

> You now see up and down the country a people better nourished, better dressed, better in health and more attractive in appearance and, I would also claim, of keener general intelligence than this country has ever shown before, credit must be given to this unprecedented effort of high salesmanship, more thoughtful and colourful marketing, in which complex operation the main force is, beyond all question or dispute, the astonishing power of bold and persuasive advertising.

No one could be more proud of their profession! It was, perhaps, fitting that his memorial service was held in St. Martin-in-the-Fields, just down from his office where he had held sway for so many years.

Although none of the sons could emulate the father, their names rarely occurring in the press or attached to any particular campaign, it would not seem that their presence in the agency was merely a matter of inheritance, for they did, eventually, hold senior management positions, and Anthony, actually co-authored a book on the work of one of the agency's subsidiaries, *Outdoor Advertising*.

Whatever contribution Sykes' sons may have made, it was Major George Harrison who was to be key to the agency's growth in the inter-war years. That he was a man of character was proven even before he joined LPE, is suggested by his receiving an M.C. & BAR in WWI. Harrison joined the agency in 1920 as assistant secretary, but such was his effectiveness, that, not three years later, he had a seat on the Board, and, by 1930, was Managing Director.

It was Harrison who took on the role of Chairman on Sykes' death, a position he was to hold along with that of Managing Director; and when he retired as Managing Director in 1951 he continued in his Chairmanship until 1961. It was Harrison who not only was key to the company's growth but who initiated its 'scientific' consumer research surveys, making LPE the birthplace, cradle and nursery of Market Research in this country.

His industry showed recognition of his commitment by awarding him the Advertising Association's Macintosh Medal; LPE showed its gratitude by commissioning Jacob Epstein to sculpt him. And when a group of advertising men decided to set up an archive, celebrating the history of advertising, the History of Advertising Trust, it was Harrison who was to be its first Chairman.

The organizational structure of LPE, as it developed under Sykes and Harrison, was a complicated one, unlike that of any other advertising agency. It established a group of six subsidiary companies, each run autonomously, but each servicing the main organization. Its' market research subsidiary became known as Research Services Ltd; Publicity Arts (along with the absorbed printing company The Fanfare Press and Virgo Studios) was responsible for design; Outdoor Publicity Ltd. for hoardings and other outdoor sites; Intam Ltd. dealt with overseas advertising; St. James Advertising & Publicity Co. restricted itself to financial advertising commissions and located itself in the City; and then there was the Technical & General Advertising Agency Ltd. LPE was to spread up St. Martins Lane into the City, and even into Mayfair.

When Ford tasked its London based advertising manager, Robert Adams, with recommending an agency, he is said to have approached LPE somewhat apprehensively as a 'ghastly octopus' – actually estimating some fourteen semi-autonomous companies! *The Persuasion Industry* recounts Adams increasing understanding of what the organizational structure was all about:

> The object of breaking the agency into specialist companies was simply to attract as much business as possible. If firms did not want LPE to do their advertising they could still use St James's Advertising to place their company reports in the financial press, or get brochures printed at the Fanfare Press or get advice on what they should pay their salesmen from Marketing & Market Development… 'a splendid machine for making money'.

From the early 1920s LPE also had a group already working on commercials to be displayed on film, known, at one time, as the Industrial & Educational Film Co. Ltd. By 1925 it was noted:

> Their film service had produced and exhibited advertisement films for over fifty clients in upward of two thousand cinemas in Great Britain and Ireland.

And then when commercial radio arrived, and after that commercial television, LPE expanded rapidly into those markets as well. It was to nurture a number of specialists for the field, two names particularly standing out for their post-LPE careers, building on their early experiences at LPE – Howard Thomas and Keith Lucas.

Thomas had been a copywriter with F.C. Pritchard Wood & Partners when he had come to LPE's notice for his work for the *Manchester Guardian*; an offer was made, and he was tempted away. At LPE he morphed from copywriter to producer, putting radio commercials together and placing them in such outlets as Radio Luxembourg. With the onset of war advertising work was dwindling and Thomas left to join the BBC, later to further develop his distinguished career as Head of Pathe News and then at Thames Television, (as well as being the man who discovered Vera Lynn).

Lucas, although an artist by training, studying at the Royal College, was actually taken on by LPE as a copywriter, albeit he was drawn into some design work. He was later to become Professor of Film and Television at the Royal College of Art, Director of the British Film Institute, and then Head of Radio, Film and Television Studies at what is now the University of Canterbury, in his home county. *Art & Industry* in 1953, wrote of LPE as it was by then:

> If, as Voltaire suggested, God is on the side of the big battalions, it may be worth mentioning that the total staff of The London Press Exchange Ltd. and its group of companies is some six hundred people.

ARTISTS & DESIGNERS

LPE drew its artists and designers from a variety of sources. Soon after it was founded there sprang up in Britain what were referred to as 'artists' studios' – an entrepreneur, frequently himself an artist, retained other artists, to form a 'stable' to be drawn upon, appropriate to each new commission arriving. One of the earliest of these to be established, in 1902, the Carlton Studios, had been set up by a group of young Canadian artists, to be followed, soon after, by the likes of the Norfolk Studios, the Brockhurst Studios, Gossop's studio, and a flood of others.

LPE was to commission artists from a number of these, as, for example, making use of Eric Fraser from Gossop's studio for Mr. Therm and for other clients. The Studio it seems to have made most use of was Clement Dane, possibly because it was nearby, on The Strand. Founded in the 1920s it became known for its design of large lithographic posters and for its work for London Transport. It would advertise itself as offering 'Modern Art for the Business Man'. LPE appears to have used it continually from the 1930s for advertisements for Reckitt & Colman, the Brewer Society and The Timber Development Council, through to the 1950s with LPE's campaign for *The Times*. In the 1950s a new Studio, to be a particular favourite of LPE, was The Artist Partners Limited, one of whose founders was Reginald Mount, renowned for his posters for the Government during WWII. Founded in 1950, it expanded rapidly to retain some fifty artists including Hans Unger who LPE was to use for a number of clients including Cadburys.

CLEMENT DANE STUDIO

190 STRAND W·C·2   PHONE: CITY 4289

Opposite: Advertisement for Clement Dane Studio, an artists' studio used by LPE.

Above: 'Keep Death Off The Road' poster, c.1957. Art Directed by Phillip Boydell and illustrated by William Little.

Of course LPE had its own stable of artists, albeit it is not clear who actually employed any one artist for a commission when Publicity Arts became 'associated' with LPE. Publicity Arts had been founded by an ex-Slade student, H.E. Collett, and, like the Clement Dane Studio, it was nearby on The Strand. When it became a LPE subsidiary it was moved to a purpose-built studio in St. Martin's Lane. LPE was also to absorb The Fanfare Press, started in 1925 by the Manchester advertising entrepreneur C.W. Hobson. He had wanted to bring his Press to London to be run by Beatrice Warde and Stanley Morison of the Monotype Corporation but, when frustrated in this, he sold it to LPE in 1926 who by this inherited a master printer, Ernest Ingham, who, fortunately, continued to be advised by Morison.

The one artist who was clearly employed by LPE was Phillip Boydell, who joined the agency in 1926, and was to stay loyally with it through to 1961, rising to become Art Director with a seat on the Board. Boydell, born in Tyldesley, in Lancashire, in 1896, started his art training at the Manchester School of Art and later, after his service in WWI, moved on to the Royal College of Art. After a few years as an art teacher he was taken on by LPE, and such was his ability that within a year of his joining, *Commercial Art*, the major journal on graphic design at the time, was referring to him as 'the thinker', 'the man with ideas'.

This view of Boydell was reaffirmed when the advertising woman extraordinaire, Mary Gowing, included Boydell in her

Opposite, left: LPE press advertisements for Three Nuns. Centre three adverts by Phillip Boydell, others by A.R. Thomson, c. 1929.

Opposite, right: Art Direction by Phillip Boydell, with drawing by Pierre Monnerat, c. 1957.

series of articles for *Art & Industry* in 1957, under the title 'The Creative Mind in Advertising'. She quoted one of Boydell's subordinates describing him, 'He has more energy and more mental energy than any man has the right to have.'

Boydell seems to have used this creative energy beyond LPE when acting as President of the Advertising Creative Circle, developing a scheme for work placement in agencies for art school students during their holidays. His book *The Artist in Advertising*, aimed at students, was to be set up by those at the Camberwell School of Art.

As much design in advertising is usually put out anonymously it is often difficult to ascribe any particular image to any one artist. For example the notorious poster for a road safety campaign, 'The Black Widow', which so horrified the public it had eventually to be withdrawn, is ascribed to Boydell, and although he did act as art director for it, the actual illustration was by William Little. Sometimes, when Boydell's name does appear, the caption might add a qualification as with LPE's advertisement for Cadbury's Crunchie Bar where it is described as 'initiated and planned by Phillip Boydell'.

Among Boydell's many successes at LPE was his Squander Bug for the Government's wartime savings campaign. Such became his design reputation that his typeface was used as 'official' for all Festival of Britain publicity – thin letters in a sans serif font with a three-dimensional appearance – it was only available in capitals.

Opposite, left: Boydell's Festival of Britain typeface, c. 1951.

Opposite, right: Festival poster prepared by LPE, featuring Boydell's typeface, 1951.

Above: Poster for Super National Benzole, by F.H.K. Henrion, 1960s.

A guide was available for the Festival designers use of it, and after the Festival it was made available for general use.

Over the years LPE was to use some of the now remembered most notable artists and designers of the time as, for example, in the 1930s and '40s, the London Transport 'poster girl' Dora Batty, the society artist Anna Zinkeisen, Stephen Spurrier, the Royal Academician, C.F. Tunnicliffe , the wildlife illustrator, and the scraper board genius T.L. Poulter; and, in the post-war years, George Him, F.H.K. Henrion and Abram Games.

Above: Advertisement for the Brewers' Society, with drawings by T.L. Poulton, 1930s.

Above right: Press advertisement for Boots, with artwork by C.F. Tunnicliffe, 1940s.

Opposite: Two from a series of advertisements for Reckitt's bath cubes, c. 1929.

Where's Father?

Not downstairs! Not in his room! Gracious! is the man still in that bath! Helped himself to one of those bath cubes I suppose.

Yes—Father has discovered how Reckitt's Bath Cubes soften hard water, how they take the harsh edge off the water, how they make the water all satin and sympathy. And then they make the water very fragrant and they give tone and tonic to the skin. A whole cube for the bath and just a pinch for a shave. Father knows that too!

Reckitt's Bath Cubes can be obtained at all Grocers Stores, etc. at 2d. each or in dainty cartons of six for 1/-

RECKITT'S BATH CUBES

Essence of Flowers   Lavender & Verbena

RECKITT AND SONS LTD   HULL AND LONDON

And she didn't leave the office till quarter-to-seven

¶ *Felt almost too tired to go out again — told Mother so. But she turned on the hot water and had a bath. Added one of her Reckitt's Bath Cubes.*

Just a simple thing to remember and to do. But what a blessing! Turning each and every bath you have into a real tonic! Giving you such a smooth and supple skin. Such calm confident nerves. Such radiance. Such physical rightness. Have you tried the luxury of Reckitt's Bath Cubes?

RECKITT'S bath cubes

2d. EACH or in dainty cartons of SIX for 1/-

¶ ALL GROCERS AND STORES SELL THEM IN 4 PERFUMES — *Lily of the Valley, Lavender Verbena & Essence of Flowers* · · · Reckitt & Sons, Ltd., Hull and London

SAMPLE ADVERTS

Over the years, LPE was to carry out commissions from a vast number of clients, spread across industries, not choosing, as some agencies to develop a speciality in any one, as, for example CPV for fashion or Higham's for technology. In the mid-1920s Percy Bradshaw, in his book on art and advertising, listed some of LPE's clients at the time to illustrate its stretch – Kodak, Barclay's Lager, Cadbury's, Steinway, the British Commercial Gas Association, Daimler Hire and Horlicks. Here are some examples.

1922

1928

1929

1940

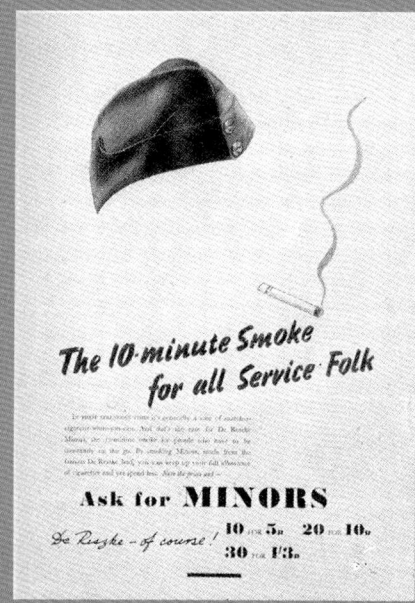
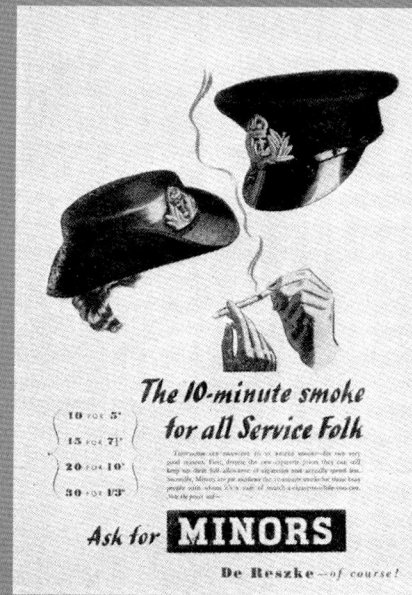

1953

The coloured gaiety of an Edwardian evening preserved within the greyer world of today... The interval's little valley of relaxed small-talk between the towering peaks of music and emotion... The crispness of a white tie seen against a fat background, all crimson and gold... And for perfection one thing more—

NUMBER SEVEN —by ABDULLA

Abdulla 'Virginia' No. 7, 20 for 3/11

ABDULLA & COMPANY LIMITED · 173 NEW BOND STREET · LONDON · W1

1941

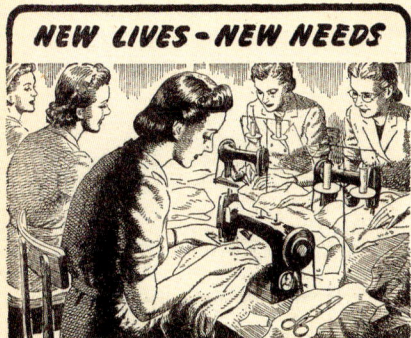

NEW LIVES – NEW NEEDS

Beauty-culture girl *sews battledresses*

Her skilful young hands used to be adept with creams and clever make-up. Now they're busy amid the whirr of machines, shaping the rough khaki cloth. From a fashionable beauty salon to a clothing factory — that's a pretty tough change, requiring from these girls new reserves of stamina, new ability to 'take it'.

ON the Home Front, battles are being won every day — big little victories over tiredness, irritability, nervous strain. Nature's own tonic, sound *natural* sleep (whenever you can get it) is the best thing ever for your new wartime lives. A warming cup of Bourn-vita, *still at the old peacetime price*, will help you to get your essential ration of body-and-mind-restoring SLEEP. Bourn-vita is a night food-drink with special nerve-soothing properties that bring sleep very quickly.

See panel for analysis of Bourn-vita.

WHY BOURN-VITA SLEEP IS RESTORING SLEEP

Phosphorus Calcium, Iron	Mineral and nerve foods
Malt Extract	Tonic and digestive properties
Calcium Vitamins A, B and D	Essential to the body's health

NO SUGAR NEEDED

GET THE BEST OUT OF YOUR SLEEP WITH—

CADBURY'S **BOURN-VITA**
1/5 PER ½ LB   STILL AT PRE-WAR PRICE

The "Go To It!" theme inspires the example shown above and that on the opposite page. *This Page: Advertiser*: Cadbury's. *Agents*: London Press Exchange Ltd. *Right: Advertiser*: Vine Products Ltd. *Agents*: Service Advertising Ltd.

1940s

1953

1930

c.1935

1928

1928

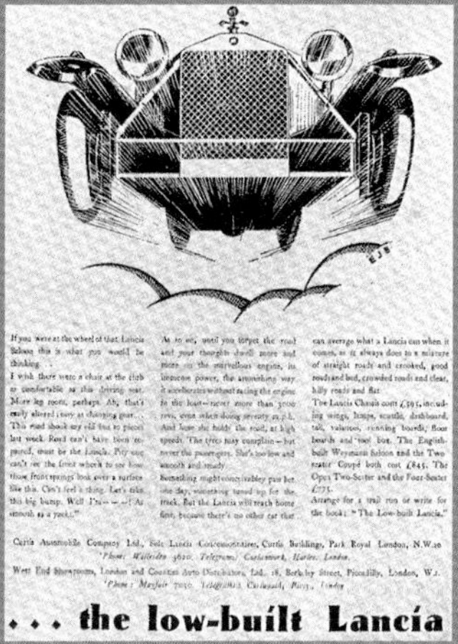

1931

c. 1940

When Jack Frost paralyses your pistons
and the handle's got to do what the battery won't
YOU HAVE BEEN WARNED!
It's time you got an

BATTERY
'Still keeps going when the rest have stopped'

Turning that handle is a knuckle-dusting job. Why keep a battery and bark yourself? Chuck it away! Chuck away the handle too! Go now and get an Exide. You know — the battery that nine out of ten British ships at sea rely on — that battery that *still keeps going when the rest have stopped.*
★ There are Exide batteries for every model of every make of car, at prices to suit every pocket — from any of the 600 Exide Service Stations.

THE CHLORIDE ELECTRICAL STORAGE CO. LTD., (Exide and Drydex Batteries), EXIDE WORKS, CLIFTON JUNCTION, Nr. MANCHESTER
Also at London, Manchester, Birmingham, Bristol, Glasgow, and Belfast

c. 1964

BIG-CAR MOTORING at small-car costs!

300,000 buyers in 16 months make Cortina Britain's biggest seller. In races and rallies everywhere, Cortina versions gallop away with the prizes. Why all this success? Cortina performance is striking — up to 80 mph fast. With graceful looks and easy room for five. Tough dependability. Low first cost and up to 40 mpg. Test-drive Cortina and see! From only £573. 6s. 3d. tax paid.

CORTINA FROM FORD

c.1961

1934   c.1960   c.1962

1930

AVRO FIVE

1931

Strong head winds.... only 4 hours petrol.... in touch with Berengaria.... Wireless working well.... Position please?

c. 1960

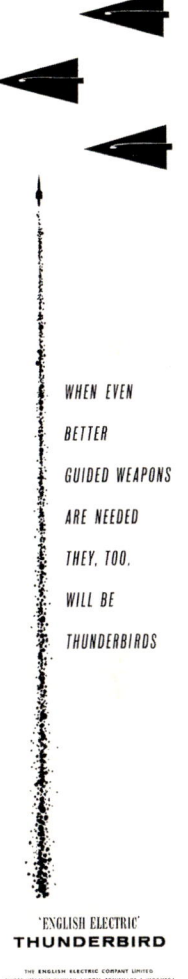

WHEN EVEN BETTER GUIDED WEAPONS ARE NEEDED THEY, TOO, WILL BE THUNDERBIRDS

'ENGLISH ELECTRIC'
THUNDERBIRD

CONSUMER RESEARCH

Mark Abrams, LPE pioneer of consumer research, c. 1957.

LPE stood apart from other agencies in what seems to have been a highly effective, albeit complex, operational structure; but it actually stood out, deserving to be given iconic status in the advertising industry, for the operation of one of its subsidiaries, the rather stolid dull sounding Research Services Ltd., for it was this unit that was to be the birthplace and nursery of British market (consumer) research.

Although the name Mark Abrams will, forever, be associated with the development of consumer research in this country, when he joined LPE in 1933 he later admitted he knew very little, if anything, about the subject. With a doctorate in modern English economic history from the London School of Economics, he had drifted across the Atlantic, in 1931, to take up a place as a research fellow at the Brookings Institute in Washington. Two years later he returned to Britain jobless and aimless. Via the grapevine he heard that LPE was looking for a researcher and he was offered and accepted the post.

But LPE was already thinking consumer research before his arrival. *Commercial Art* had written of Sykes in his early days in advertising as 'setting out to investigate a situation from his office, to ask questions of shop keepers and individuals'. Percy Bradshaw wrote of the agency in the mid-1920s:

> But it is evident that, long before the writing and designing of an advertisement is commenced, this agency has

LPE research investigator badge.

invariably analysed the manufacturing and sales problems in a very complete way, distribution and its possibilities have been considered, the attitude of the trade and public has been visualized and anticipated as far as possible, the activities of competitors, and other general factors have all been judged.

And *Art & Industry* in 1953 recorded, 'Research is no new toy to the London Press Exchange Ltd. We are, we have been, for many years steeped in it.'

LPE, from its start, was the most information based of all the advertising agencies of its time; after all, Sykes came from a reporting background. And it was Major George Harrison who invited Abrams to join LPE's already well established research group, not Abrams bringing to LPE his ideas on consumer surveying; it was Harrison who was to become Chairman of the Finance and General Purpose Committee of the Audit Bureau of Circulation; and it was Harrison who became the first Chairman of the steering committee which inaugurated the television industry's audience measurement service; in 1961 he co-authored *The Home Market*, a book on the British public as consumers. *The Illustrated London News* recorded of the Major, 'he did much to further the application of research to consumer behaviour'.

Be that as it may, the research that Harrison invited Abrams to head was not a mere whisper of what was to come, but a

Right: *The Home Market*, book co-authored by George Harrison, 1936.

Far right: *Social Surveys and Social Action*, book authored by Mark Abrams for Heinemann's Contemporary Science Series, 1951.

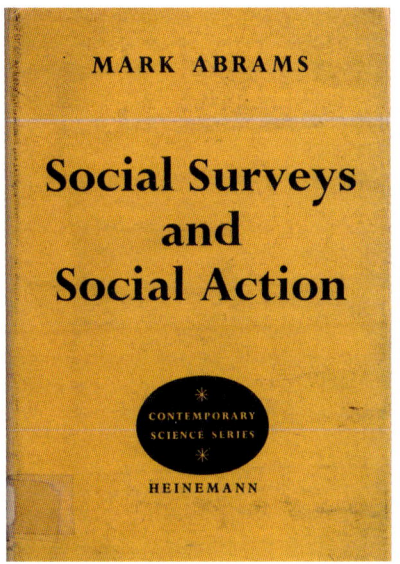

full-scale model to be followed and refined; and the youthful Abrams, at that time, more motivated by money than intellectual curiosity, 'I thought this is real money at last after coaching students at half a crown an hour.'

Harrison wanted Abrams to manage a survey of the readers of the British press – to carry out the first national readership survey. Nothing daunted, Abrams quickly swung into action. Interviewers were dispatched nationwide, each carrying a set of the previous days national newspapers, about nine. Interviewees were asked which they had read, upon which the interviewers would get them to recall what they had looked at, what they had actually read, what they had thought, and so on, page by page.

A typical LPE advertisement for Fry's Milk Punch, reflecting Abrams' concept of the teenage consumer. Initiated and planned by Boydell, 1957.

The size of the project was extraordinary, some twenty thousand interviewees, the results published in some nine volumes. The most minute details could be abstracted from the collected data, as readers of the *Daily Herald* (the major working-class paper of the time), were more likely to look at a political story if it were on the front page left-hand side; or people were much more likely to read an article in the *News Chronicle* if it were signed by the author. Some twenty years later, in 1956, this original survey was to provide a model when interested bodies (the Institute of Practitioners in Advertising, the Newspaper Publishers' Association and the Periodical Publishers' Association) set up a joint National Readership Survey covering some two hundred and fifty major national newspapers and periodicals.

As a result of the LPE survey its research subsidiary attracted a flood of commissions, from a wide range of organisations, as to how their potential customers might behave. When Abrams returned to LPE after a wartime break at the BBC Overseas Research Department and the Government Psychological Warfare Board, the research department became an independent subsidiary, Research Services Ltd, which, by the 1960s, was to grow to employ some ninety staff and to carry out literally hundreds of client surveys each year.

These could range from small specific ones as J. Arthur Rank wanting advice on how to publicise its film 'Hamlet' – (push Lawrence Olivier and Jean Simmonds and downplay Shakespeare); to ones affecting a whole industry, when the Gas, Light & Coke

LPE helps the Labour campaign, 1964.

Company sought advice on how to get customers to stay with gas and not switch to electricity. Not infrequently Abrams' subsidiary would be carrying out surveys for competitors in the same industry as for Shell and National Benzole, or for *The Times* and the *Manchester Guardian* (getting the latter to drop the word Manchester).

An example of LPE's thoroughness when given an advertising commission, is its work with Ford. It mounted a series of surveys on how people liked their cars, whatever the brand, and what they would be looking for in their next purchase. With any new model launch there would be surveys of people visiting showrooms, of new model 'awareness', of early buyers, and of that model's image in the eyes of the public; and surveys would continue throughout the first year of any particular launch to evaluate the effectiveness of the advertising for it.

Abrams seems to have been prepared to take on any issue that was brought to him that could be clarified by a survey, from a Labour party election campaign to how a European market might respond. The Archive Centre at Churchill College, Cambridge, which holds some of Abrams' material, describes that part covering surveys as being for newspapers, retailers, and manufacturers, universities, trade unions, new town planners, charities, broadcasters and politicians!

It was this volume of survey work that provided the experience for Abrams to hone the tools for social surveying, as, for example, developing the ABC classification of social class, and the use of small groups led by psychologists for collecting data. It was as a result of his surveys that he coined the concept 'teenage consumer', a new focus for advertising, which had preciously been targeted at adults. Adams was to publish a number of books on his speciality, including *Social Surveys and Social Action* (1951) and *The Teenage Consumer* (1959). Adams, arriving at LPE largely ignorant of surveying, was to add to LPE's reputation by becoming the crusader of the subject, and was rewarded by LPE by being appointed its youngest ever director.

Such was the reputation of LPE's research group that it was in its office in St. Martin's Lane, in 1946, that the British Market Research Society was founded, Abrams being one of its twenty-three founding members. He continued to carry the banner at LPE until he left, in 1970, to become Director of the Government's Survey Research Unit of the Social Science Research Council.

SAMPLE CAMPAIGNS

Mr. Mercury

'Oh, Mr. Mercury, where should I have been without you?', LPE advertisement for National Benzole Mixture, 1937.

By the turn of the twentieth century the arrival of the combustion engine brought some hundred thousand cars on to the British roads. This, inevitably, introduced a new area for advertising, for the cars themselves and for the products essential to their running – petrol and its various additives. Shell not only dominated the petrol market but its related advertising set a standard when it came to design. Technically there was little to choose between one brand of petrol and another so it fell to advertising and publicity to make a brand stand out. In this Shell won hands down, its Shell logo to be seen everywhere; and, with its appointment of Jack Beddington and the stable of artists he sponsored, its advertising was the most frequently illustrated in the design press.

In the specialist area of motor racing, drivers found their cars ran more efficiently with ethyl alcohol or benzole, and gradually the notion was adopted for public motoring. It was LPE that National Benzole retained to distinguish its own brand, and, in 1928, it introduced the character Mr. Mercury. Mercury, mythologically, not only represented commerce and commercial gain, but was the traveller, the swift messenger of the Gods. The head of LPE's Mr. Mercury became National Benzole's trademark and his figure appeared in all its press advertising, along with such slogans as 'easy starting' and 'more miles to the gallon'.

Some considered the frisson accompanying the appearance of Mr. Mercury's nude body (many of the drivers in the advertisements being women), a unique selling point, but it was the increased

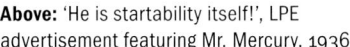

Above: 'He is startability itself!', LPE advertisement featuring Mr. Mercury, 1936.

Right: 'Oh, Mr. Mercury you did give me a start!', LPE advertisement, 1937.

'Well I never, Mr. Mercury, you did give me a start!', LPE advertisement for National Benzole Mixture, 1938.

personalization of Mr. Mercury, brought down from the heavens, sitting alongside the driver, offering him or her his support, that seems to have endeared the figure to the public. 'Oh Mr. Mercury, where should I have been without you', and, punning, 'Well I never Mr. Mercury, you did give me a start', were the ballooned drivers' responses to the increasingly humanized figure. *Art & Industry* wrote of the campaign in 1938:

> But all the time the standard of layout was getting better with the current series (the best in many people's view) Mr. Mercury, though still a shade, takes his place by the driver and starts the engine.

The fun LPE was having with the emblem is perhaps hinted at when one advertisement had Mr. Mercury actually sitting alongside Mr. Therm in the car. Mr. Mercury, as the Shell of Shell, was to appear everywhere, as in LPE's publicity booklets for National Benzole illustrated by John Dronsfield. However it was Shell who won out in the end, when it absorbed the company in the 1950s, albeit the brand was continued through to the '90s, Mr. Mercury being refashioned by Reginald Mount.

Oh, Mr. Mercury, you did give me a START!

Mr. Therm and Mr. Mercury are very close relations. The same ton of coal that gives 75 therms of gas gives also $2\frac{1}{2}$ gallons of National Benzole — the most powerful motor-spirit known, and a natural anti-knock fuel as well. Support your own industry, and give your car a treat, by running always on National Benzole Mixture—for greater startability, smoother running, and more miles per gallon

NATIONAL BENZOLE MIXTURE
The spirit of British Coal

Opposite: Advertisement for National Benzole combining Mr. Mercury and Mr. Therm, 1938.

Above: 'Mr. Mercury will give you more miles per gallon', *Courier* magazine, 1951.

Above right: 'Benzole makes good petrol better', *Courier* magazine, 1953.

Right: 'There's nothing like Super National for Winter Motoring', 1960s.

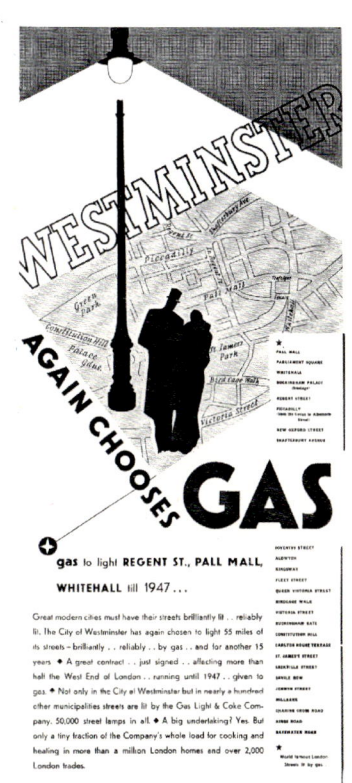

LPE press advertisement for gas before the introduction of Mr. Therm, c. 1932.

The first gas works in Britain were built by the Gas, Light & Coke Company in 1812. Initially supplying coal gas to London, over the years the company expanded, buying up smaller companies, until, by the mid-twentieth century, it was supplying gas to many millions across the whole of the South East. The gas industry was continuously competing with the electric, and when it came to the necessary advertising was dealing with a substance not easy to present in an eye-catching way to the general public.

The Gas, Light & Coke company were already making use of LPE when its publicity manager, A.P. Ryan commissioned it to produce some novelty that would put gas a step or two ahead of its rival. LPE brought in Eric Fraser. There is a hint, in some biographies of Fraser that it was not his most welcomed commission, that he was to design under pressure, albeit he was to produce what was to become one of the most iconic characters in twentieth century British advertising – Mr. Therm, who arrived on the scene in 1932.

Fraser is reported to have been paid five guineas for his first sketch of Mr. Therm, but, after some negotiating, received twenty-five guineas for later appearances. It was possibly this that led LPE to use other less expensive artists, some from its own studio, to produce some of the later Mr. Therms, and designers were to tell of their delight in reproducing the 'engaging mannekin' in a wide variety of settings. If Fraser had been at all reluctant initially he was said to have been appalled at the 'corruption' of his creation, albeit

'My Comfort Crusade', Mr. Therm arrives in a nursery themed advertisement, c. 1934.

A futile attempt by the Electrical Development Association to outdo Mr. Therm with their own character, 1936.

Mr. Therm still hyping gas in the 1960s, *Homes and Gardens* magazine, 1960.

as Sylvia Beckemeyer in her book on Fraser pointed out, 'no doubt the advertising agency failed to see the subtle differences between Fraser's drawings and those of the studio artists'.

For some thirty years Mr. Therm was to be seen everywhere – in press advertisements, on hoardings, animated, even on playing cards – he was to become synonymous with the whole of the gas industry when LPE allowed the British Commercial Gas Association (a cooperative body representing every branch of the industry) to use him.

Art & Industry was effusive in its praise, describing Mr. Therm's first appearance as 'like a blast of trumpets'; and still, into the 1940s, describing the little fellow as having 'won the hearts of the humblest and highest in the land'. Mr. Therm was only retired with the arrival of North Sea Gas, when it was judged a new, more contemporary image was required.

Left: 'Mr. Therm burns to serve you', press advert issued by the Gas Council, 1953.

Above: 'I freeze in silence', press advert issued by the Gas Council, *Punch* magazine, 1954.

'H stands for Health', press advert issued by the Gas Council, 1956.

'You'll bless the day Gas came to stay', press advert issued by the Gas Council, 1959.

The Squander Bug

LPE advertisement for the National Savings Committee, with the squander bug enticing shoppers, *Punch* magazine, 1943.

Commercial advertising commissions began to dry up with the onset of WWII, with paper and print rationing and manufacturers turning to munitions work. For many agencies it was the Government who was to come to their rescue with the establishment of the Ministry of Information, and its, and other Ministries, need to get information and instruction out to the public, whether on hoardings, in the press or in leaflets.

Governments are forever short of money, no more so than in wartime. In 1915, in WWI, the British government set up a National Savings Committee to discourage wasteful spending that might otherwise contribute to the war effort. With Charles Higham, the super confident advertising man, on the Committee, a campaign was launched to encourage the buying of savings certificates. This seems to have been sufficiently successful for people to continue the savings habit in peacetime and those with only small sums to set aside could buy saving stamps which, when accumulated to a certain sum, could be converted into certificates.

Come WWII, the Committee became high profile again, turning to some half dozen advertising agencies to get its savings message across; but its endless warnings on mindless spending appear to have gone unheeded. There was a masculine arrogance to much of what was being put out, as women, in particular, were targeted, not only the possibly profligate housewife but the many women replacing men away in the services, receiving their own wages for the first time, with that luxury possibly going to their heads.

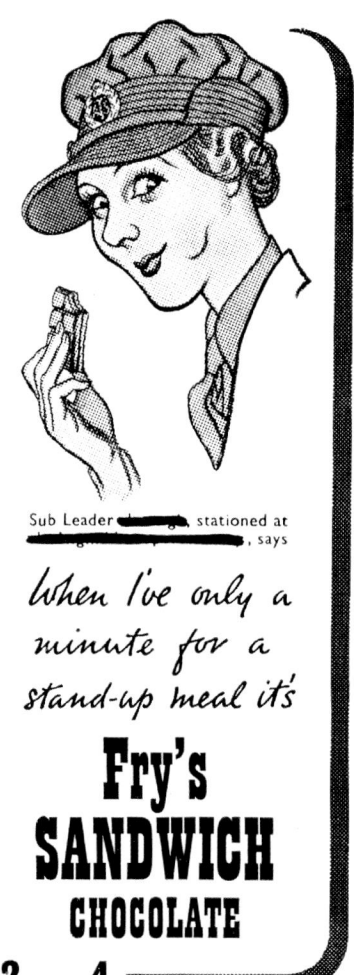

Left: Typical wartime press advertisments by LPE for Cadburys Bourn-vita (1940) and Fry's Sandwich Chocolate (1944).

Opposite: Phillip Boydell's squander bug in action in a press advertisement for the National Savings Committee, 1944.

LPE, like so many other advertising agencies in wartime, had amended their peacetime advertisements to patriotic ones – people appeared in uniform, women were featured not in the kitchen but in munition factories – and the captions followed – for Clarke's soup 'I'm going to heat up the soup before the warning goes', or for Peek Freen 'lightweight meals for night-long raids'; it was already tuned in to the wartime zeitgeist.

The National Savings Committee turned to LPE to think up some way of encouraging the purchasing of non-essentials to be reduced and the investment in war savings to be increased. In 1943 the Squander Bug was introduced to the nation. LPE's Boydell initially produced half a dozen sketches of a creature he named the Money Grub, providing both the captions and the layout. Much has been made of Boydell being ill with flu at the time he produced an image that was to go worldwide. Although the creature's name was changed to the Squander Bug it remained much as Boydell had originally conceived it. He said that he had created it so that it could be activated in any way in any situations – it had to be able to push, pull, scratch, steal and bite.

The Squander Bug began to appear in the press, accompanied by speech balloons encouraging people to waste their money on useless purchases, 'more wages this week, you can buy lots of useless trash'.

Such enticement would be accompanied by the Government's direction to put the specimen out of action, it being 'Hitler's Pal':

MAKE DO AND MEND AND YOU'LL "DO" HIM TOO!

The Squander Bug hates needles and cotton! He wants you to buy new clothes instead of making your old ones last even longer, and saving coupons. Don't listen to him... your needle is a weapon of war to-day... see that it works full time! With the money saved buy Savings Stamps or Certificates.

Savings Certificates costing 15/- are worth 20/6 in 10 years—increase free of income tax. They can be bought outright, or by instalments with 6d., 2/6 or 5/- Savings Stamps through your Savings Group or Centre or at any Post Office or Trustee Savings Bank. Buy now!

ISSUED BY THE NATIONAL SAVINGS COMMITTEE

Those Savings Stamps are precious to you, they represent the price of things you have willingly gone without. Don't let the Squander Bug undo all your good work now. See that your stamps are invested so as to benefit you as well as the country.

★

Use your Stamps to buy Savings Certificates, or to increase your deposit at the Post Office or a Trustee Savings Bank

Far left: 'Make do and mend and you'll "do" him too!', press advertisement with the squander bug, *Sunday Pictorial*, 1943.

Left: Boydell's squander bug in action, *Housewife* magazine, 1944.

An American version of the squander bug said to stem from the pen of Dr Seuss.

'Don't listen to the Squander bug'
'Kill that pest'
'Squash the Squander Bug'
'Don't take the Squander Bug with you when you go shopping'

The 'symbolic tempter' was soon taken up by and played with by a whole range of cartoonists. Mary Gowing recorded, 'Vicki, Grimes, George Whitelaw, Zec, Giles, Neb, Strube, Low… there was not a cartoonist who did not exploit the Squander Bug.'

There was soon an American version, said to stem from the pen of Dr Seuss, with such captions as 'Starve the Squander Bug. Buy war bonds', the bug portrayed eating dollar bills; whilst the Australians had the bug with Japanese features. The Bug appeared not only in the Press, but on hoardings, in animated cartoons, and there was even a version in Madame Tussauds.

Such was the impact of Boydell's bug that by the end of the war the Government was said to have had to employ over a thousand civil servants to service its saving scheme.

Double Diamond's Little Man

An examples of LPE's pre-WWII drinks advertising for Barclay's Lager, 1931.

It was not really until the 1930s that beer drinking began to shift up the social scale from the working to the middle classes; and not until after WWII that a branded beer became a national phenomenon rather than just being sold regionally.

From the late nineteenth century a small Burton-on-Trent brewery, Allsop & Sons, began to grow to become a global giant, largely aided by its pale ale, Double Diamond. The history of the company, from 1934 known as Inde Coop & Allsop Ltd. through a merger, was to be, indeed, virtually the history of Double Diamond. It was one of the first beers to 'go national', becoming, by the late 1950s the best selling beer on the British market. Pre-war advertising for it was unremarkable, but come the late 1940s, with other national beers as competitors, brand advertising became essential. Enter the 'little hat man'.

LPE was already well-experienced with working for the drinks industry with its pre-war commissions for the likes of Barclay's Lager and the lengthy campaign in the latter half of the 1930s for the Brewers' Society 'beer is best'. *Commercial Art* had particularly praised this latter, 'The campaign succeeds in making one feel that a man's appetite for beer is a right and proper thing and good for health.'

But the pleasant rural scenes that had suited the interwar advertisements were unlikely to meet the mood of the post-war years. When LPE got the commission for Double Diamond it brought in Peter Probyn who was to provide a character for

Double Diamond—The Little Man

Right: A further example of LPE's pre-WWII work, 'Beer is best' advertisement for the Brewers' Society, 1934.

Far right: Peter Probyn's character for Double Diamond, 'Little Man'.

Opposite: Press advertisment for Double Diamond, featuring the Little Man character, 1954.

the ale that came to stand for the brand for nearly twenty years. Probyn was building a career as a cartoonist, his work to appear in nationals as *Punch*, *The Tatler* and *Lilliput*, his humour described as 'gentle'. What was, perhaps, paradoxical was that Probyn was a wine buff, a major illustrator of the Wine Society's publications, and his lips may never have even touched a Double Diamond.

Probyn's Little Man was not portrayed as everyman, the man in the street, but as a City accountant – with bowler hat, toothbrush moustache, striped trousers and rolled umbrella; boring, unadventurous. He came to be used as a brand logo, but frequently

Never go without your Double Diamond

Wherever you go (yes, even when you are travelling) you are never far from a Double Diamond. A Double Diamond *works wonders* at any time—takes the tension out of life (and travel), revives your confidence, puts you back on top of your form. The world is at its best after a Double Diamond—wherever you are!

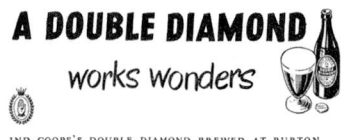

IND COOPE'S DOUBLE DIAMOND BREWED AT BURTON

he would take centre stage doing feats not to be expected of a mere number cruncher – catching a thief robbing a bank, winning the heart of a mermaid, and, for the 1953 Coronation, atop a flag pole made up of beer barrels, waving the Union Jack high above the crowds below – shades of Walter Mitty. The slogan most usually accompanying him was 'a Double Diamond works wonders'. As with the other emblems the Little Man was to appear in other guises beyond the pages of the press or on the hoardings, as, for example, when made into a figurine.

But by the early 1960s Inde Coope decided that perhaps the Little Man had run his course, and removed the account from LPE to Hobson Bates, an American owned agency originally started by the British John Bates, who had done his apprenticeship, as it were, at Colman, Prentis and Varley. Out went the little man, in came more macho images of skiers and yachtsmen and the like, along with the slogan 'the beer that men drink'; out went the Press and hoardings, in came television.

The Little Man character still lurking into the early 1960s.

'A Double Diamond works wonders', publicity from 1954.

'The Beer the men drink', the macho replacement of the Little Man, 1960s.

'Top People'

'Top people read The Times', designed by Abram Games for LPE's campaign, c. 1962.

In the early 1950s, when newsprint came off the ration, competition between national newspapers became fierce. *The Times*, with its large format, began to be concerned by its drop in circulation likely to result in its attracting less advertising. At the time LPE was its advertising agency and this led their management to commission LPE's research services to carry out a readership survey, which was done by Mark Abrams. The conclusions were that the newspaper was too large, too dull and too expensive.

The Times' management decided that at that point of time it could do little about any of these concerns, but that it would be easier to tackle the paper's image. However, in this instance, LPE's suggestions were not considered particularly imaginative. By chance Stanley Morison, then typographic consultant to *The Times*, met G.H. Saxon Mills the copywriter, and sent him the LPE readership survey. Although ageing, Saxon Mills still retained some of his old verve, 'Effective advertising need not be vulgar, but there must be red blood in it as well as blue blood.'

It was Saxon-Mills who produced the slogan 'Top People Read the Times', and went on to write the copy for the subsequent advertising campaign. LPE was retained to commission the artists, set the copy, prepare the layouts and place the advertisements; these were to appear in a host of publications as well as on hoardings.

The commissioned artists had the challenge to portray what were termed Saxon Mills 'menagerie' of characters – barristers, scientists, trade unionists, political candidates, and the like. LPE

George Him for LPE's Top People campaign, c. 1960.

Royston Cooper for LPE's Top People campaign, c. 1961

Above: George Him, 'Top People take The Times wherever they go', 1959.

Right: 'Why do seven-tenths of top dons and teachers take THE TIMES?', 1960s.

Far right: 'Top people take The Times', designed by Eric Fraser, 1960s.

was then asked to do another readership survey, which, this time, was carried out by psychologists using small groups. For the illustrations of the advertisements LPE used a number of artists, the best-known being Abram Games, George Him and Patrick Tilley. Maurice Lovell is recorded as art director. Although many sneered at the campaign, it got *The Times* noticed and was continued through until 1960.

The Times 'Top People' campaign well illustrates LPE's advantage with its Subsidiaries structure, for Times management was able to swing backwards and forwards, from one subsidiary to another without, apparently, bad feelings.

Epilogue

The London Press Exchange was unique in British advertising agencies in the first half of the twentieth century. It stood apart from the others, not merely in its size and profitability, but by its organisational structure and its emphasis on data collection.

Of the latter, from its start-up Sykes had despised 'flair' and demanded information; and when this line was taken up by Harrison and Abrams, it morphed into a new social science (new to Britain), market research. LPE became the flag bearer and proselytiser, a model that other agencies, although caught up with the concept, could not match either the LPE's commitment or its standards.

And although critics were cynical about LPE's structure of subsidiary companies, seeing it merely as a way of increasing income, it came to benefit both employees and clients. Employees had increased motivation, each subsidiary being an independent profit operation serving LPE but free to seek clients where it would; and, in addition, executives in the subsidiaries weren't just generalists but could hone up their specialism to offer a high level of service whether it was for placing an outside advertisement, advertising financial products, or acting as business consultants. And with the structure clients could pick and choose whichever service they needed, whether it was merely for printing a brochure, or placing an advertisement, or devising a complete campaign for a new brand.

Although LPE did not stand out when it came to advertising design, not hazarding the modernism of McKnight Kauffer or the playful typography of Ashley Havinden, it produced a number of

Opposite: A meeting at the London Press Exchange in St Martin's Lane, London, 1951.

brand 'characters' that were to be absorbed into the general culture of the time, some relatively short-lived, as the Squander Bug, others, as Mr. Therm and Mr. Mercury holding their popularity for decades.

By the late 1960s LPE had slipped down the pecking order of British agencies, having lost the Ford and the Worthington Beer accounts. But by then it had built up a considerable international network and it felt that this would be a good bargaining tool when it decided the best thing would be to merge with an American agency, one not strong in this respect. LPE was the first of the long-established British agencies to fall into American hands. The agency with which it merged was Leo Burnett from Chicago. Initially the new entity was titled Leo Burnett-LPE, but soon the LPE was dropped, and LPE was gone.

For readers who wish to delve deeper into the history of the London Press Exchange, related papers are held at the National Archives and at the History of Advertising Trust.